Historical Atlases of South Asia,
Central Asia, and the Middle East

A HISTORICAL ATLAS OF

IRAN

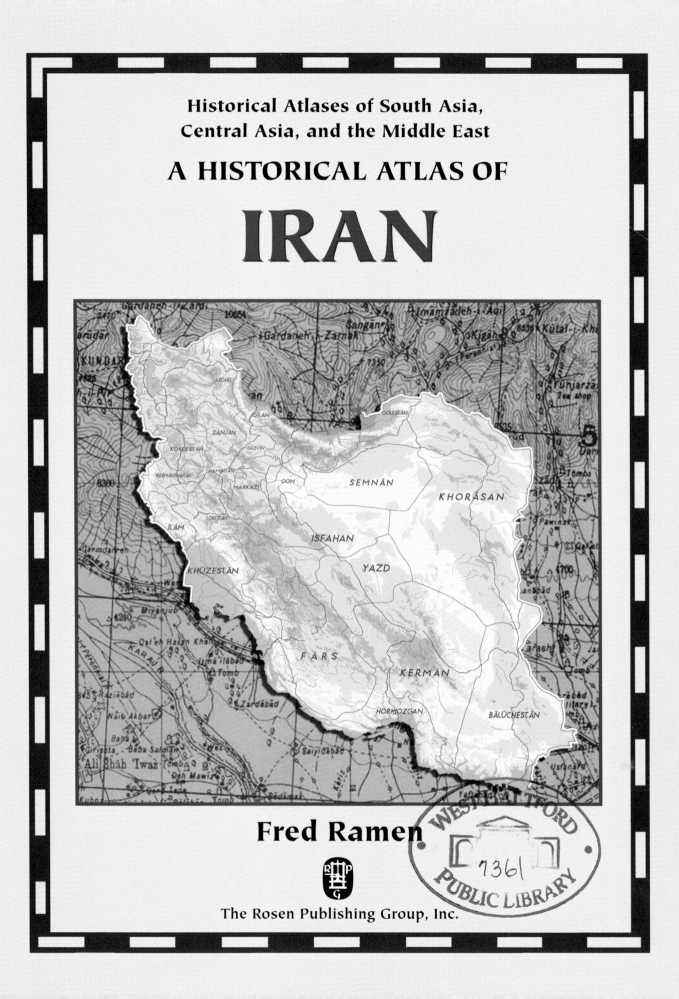

Fred Ramen

The Rosen Publishing Group, Inc.

To Allison

Published in 2003 by The Rosen Publishing Group, Inc.
29 East 21st Street, New York, NY 10010

Library of Congress Cataloging-in-Publication Data

Ramen, Fred
A Historical Atlas of Iran / Fred Ramen. — 1st ed.
    p. cm. — (Historical atlases of South Asia, Central Asia, and the Middle East)
Summary: Maps and text chronicle the history of this Middle Eastern country formerly called Persia.
Includes bibliographical references and index.
ISBN 0-8239-3864-6
1. Iran—History—Maps for children. 2. Iran—Maps for children. [1. Iran—History.
2. Atlases.] I. Title. II. Series.
G2256.S1 R3 2002
911'.55—dc21

2002031031 2002031718

Manufactured in the United States of America

Cover image: Iran, the nation formerly known as Persia, has a long, rich history. Images on this cover span from the early Sassanian Empire to the present. *Clockwise from top left*: An artifact from the Sassanian Empire, a contemporary painting of a prince from the eighteenth-century Qajar Period, and a photo of current president Mohammad Khatami.

Contents

CASPIAN SEA

TURKMENISTAN

ARDABĪL

GĪLĀN

ZANJĀN

GOLESTĀN

TEHRAN

SEMNĀN

MARKAZĪ

BAGHDAD
IRAQ
Tigris

ĪLĀM

ISFAHAN

YAZD

KHŪZESTĀN
Ahvāz

BŪSHEHR

Shīrāz

FĀRS

KERMĀN

PERSIAN GULF

QATAR

HORMOZGAN

OMAN

UNITED ARAB
EMIRATES

Gulf of
Oman

Mashhad

BĀLŪCHESTĀN

INTRODUCTION

For thousands of years, the region of present-day Iran has been one of the most important places in history. Humans lived there 100,000 years ago, most likely in caves embedded in the Elburz and Zagros mountain chains in the southeast. Archaeologists have found remains of Neanderthal man within Iran's present-day boundaries. As the first cities appeared on the Mesopotamian plain, the inhabitants of Iran settled into farming communities and walled towns. The region was an important trade link between the Mesopotamian civilizations and the civilizations of India and China. These merchant routes later became part of the Silk Road.

Since 1935, the area has been called Iran, but it has had many other names in its long history. The most common one is Persia, the name used by the ancient Greeks.

Iran's strategic location on the Persian Gulf makes it one of the most pivotal countries in the Middle East. Known as Persia until 1935, Iran became independent in 1979 and was renamed the Islamic Republic of Iran. At that time, the ruling shah was forced into exile. Iran has since been involved in several conflicts with neighboring countries, specifically Iraq, over border disputes and occupied lands. Iran's population of more than 66,130,000 people is nearly all Shiite Muslim.

Much of Iran is surrounded by mountain ranges, but the country still benefits from its two coasts—one in the north along the Caspian Sea and the other one to the south along the Persian Gulf and the Gulf of Oman. The mountainous areas of the country lie in sharp contrast to its coastal regions and offer a variety of elevations, with some peaks as high as 6,500 feet (2,000 meters). Iran is also home to several volcanoes—both active and inactive—and frequently experiences earthquakes.

In ancient times, Iran was home to great empires that rivaled the might and culture of the Greek city-states. Alexander the Great was fascinated by the Persian Empire and adopted many of its conventions. When Islam was introduced by the Arab invaders, the Iranian civilization did not vanish. Instead, it became one of the great cultural centers of the Islamic world.

Iran's terrain is hostile, with high mountain ranges towering over fierce deserts. About two-thirds of it is impossible to farm. Iran's most dominating features are its two mountain ranges, the Elburz and the Zagros, and its two deserts, the Dasht-i Kavir and the Dasht-i Lut.

Iran does have fertile land, however. One such region lies along the Caspian Sea. Khuzistan, in the southwest, has a similar climate to present-day Iraq and is an important source of food. While much of Iran is inhospitable, it does have vast reserves of oil and natural gas, the basis for much of its present economy.

The people of Iran are as diverse as its geography. Iranians, descendants of the Aryans, make up the majority of the population. The modern name of the country is derived from the ancient Persian Aryânâm, which means "land of the Aryans." Arabs, descendants of the conquering warriors who first brought Islam to Iran, and Turks, whose ancestors began moving into the region almost a thousand years ago, are Iran's two other major groups.

This diverse land has played a major role on the world's stage for more than 2,500 years. This book will explore just some of the history of this complex region.

ANCIENT IRAN

Iran, a nation located in southwestern Asia, is bordered by Iraq and Turkey to the west, and Afghanistan and Pakistan to the east. Turkmenistan, Armenia, and Azerbaijan, all formerly part of the Soviet Union, border Iran to the north, along with the Caspian Sea—considered the largest saltwater lake in the world. Iran also has access to the Persian Gulf and the Gulf of Oman in the south. Iran's proximity to warm ocean waters has made it a desirable location for centuries.

The Achaemenid Empire

About 3,500 years ago, the first Aryan peoples migrated from what is now central Asia in the north into the region of present-day Iran. The Aryans were split into a number of tribes, each of which settled in a different place. Two of the most important were the Medes, who settled in the northern and eastern sections of Iran, and the Persians, who occupied the southern sections of Iran, a region then known as Fars.

The Medes built a powerful empire and fought many wars against their neighbors, especially the Assyrians, who had conquered the Mesopotamia region throughout much of the ninth century BC. By 585 BC, the Medes had managed to destroy the Assyrian Empire and were

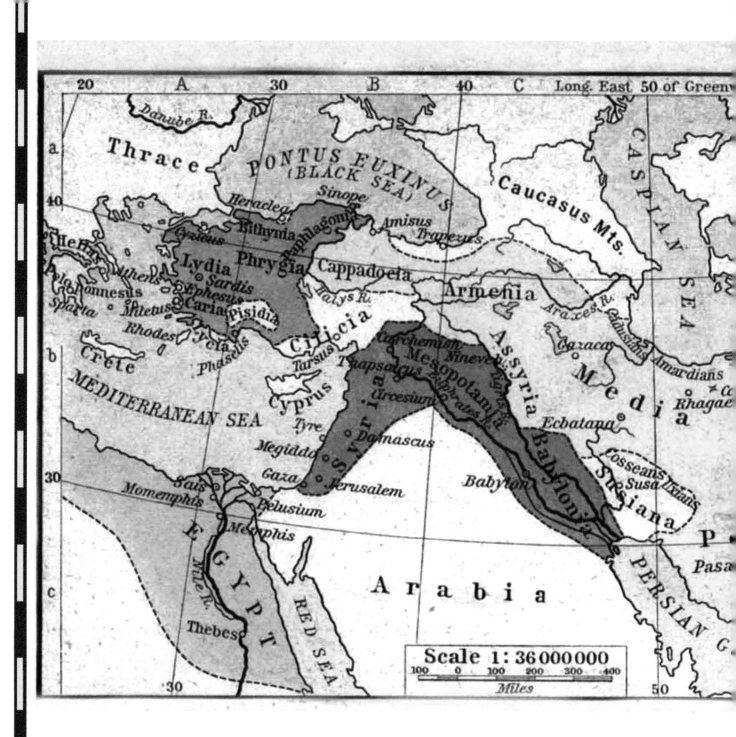

The Median Empire, shown on this historical map from 1923, most likely ruled over the Persians during the seventh century BC. About 200 years later, the Medes and Scythians united with other small groups to topple the Assyrian Empire. Cyaxares (625–585 BC), also known as Uvakhashatra, was the king who united the Median army. This army then attacked important Assyrian cities, including Arrapkha, Nineveh, and Ashur. Median armies eventually pushed fleeing Assyrians into Syria. After gaining control of much of the region, the Medes, like the Persians, entered into a war with the Lydians, the most dominant group in Asia Minor. This map first appeared in *The Historical Atlas* by William R. Shepherd.

The Oriental Empires
about 600 B.C.
- Lydian Empire
- Median Empire
- Chaldean Empire
- Egyptian Empire

Independent regions uncolored.

extending their influence throughout the Near East.

Cyrus the Great

Meanwhile, the Persians were an important subject kingdom of the Medes. Around 550 BC, their king, Cyrus II, known as Cyrus the Great (reigned 559–529 BC), led a revolt against Median power. He defeated the Median king Astyages (reigned 585–550 BC), taking him captive in the process, and proclaimed himself the king of both the Medes and the Persians. He then led the Persians in a series of wars that created the first great Persian Empire in the region.

The empire founded by Cyrus the Great is called the Achaemenid Empire, after the mythical hero Achaemenes, from whom Cyrus claimed direct descent. He led his army against Parthia in what is now eastern Iran, adding it to his territory, and then turned westward toward present-day Iraq, Syria, and Saudi Arabia. He fought a war against Lydia, present-day Turkey, the most powerful kingdom in Asia Minor, completely defeating Lydia in 547 BC. This conquest brought the Persians into contact with the Greek colonies on the coast of Asia Minor, many of which were forced to submit to Persian rule. In 539 BC, Cyrus turned to Mesopotamia, conquering Babylonia, Palestine, and Assyria and bringing the entire region under his control. During this time, he freed the Hebrews who had been enslaved by the Babylonians, allowing them to return to Jerusalem and rebuild their Temple of Solomon. Cyrus,

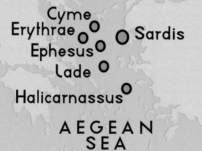

Sea of Azov

BLACK SEA

ADRIATIC SEA

Cyme
Erythrae
Ephesus
Lade
Halicarnassus
Sardis

AEGEAN
SEA

Euphrates

MEDITERRANEAN SEA

Nile

RED SEA

Cyrus the Great (580–529 BC), founder of the Achaemenid Empire, under whose reign the winged sphinxes on the above relief sculpture were designed, came from a long line of leaders. Cyrus was well respected by his people, who regarded him as "father," and even by the Greeks, a people whose territories he partially conquered. Cyrus the Great inherited the Median Empire from his grandfather Astyages, who surrendered to his son's army in 550 BC. Cyrus's conquests later included the Lydian capital of Sardis, Greek cities on the coast of the Aegean Sea, and Babylonia.

CASPIAN SEA

Babylonia

Tigris

O Pasargadae

Persian

Gulf

Gulf of
Oman

ARABIAN SEA

who is mentioned in the Book of Isaiah, is often remembered for his humanitarian efforts as he usually allowed his conquered subjects to keep their own religions.

Darius I

Cyrus's successors expanded the empire westward into Egypt and eastward into India. Darius I (reigned 522–486 BC), also known as Darius the Great, organized the empire into twenty provinces ruled by satraps, or governors. Darius conquered additional territory in the north and created roads, a postal service, and a code of laws for the entire empire. His great capital was at Persepolis in what is now southern Iran. He also came into conflict

This tapestry depicts Cyrus the Great at the Battle of Jerusalem during the city's capture in 538 BC from the Assyrians, whose king, Sennacherib, forced its inhabitants to pay heavy tributes (taxes). Cyrus permitted the Jews to return to Jerusalem and to rebuild their city and the Temple of Solomon, which were destroyed by Nebuchadrezzar about fifty years earlier.

This historical regional map of the Middle East illustrates Asian territories of the Ottoman Empire as well as neighboring countries. Created by a British engraver named Emanuel Bowen between 1744 and 1752, the latter its year of publication, it illustrates Asia Minor, including Turkey, sections of the Persian Empire (present-day Iran), the Arabian Peninsula, and Egypt. Bowen was later appointed to a position as a royal cartographer by the British monarchy.

with the Greeks, losing a small but critical battle to them at Marathon in 490 BC. His son, Xerxes I (reigned 486–465 BC), was determined to crush the Greeks and launched a massive invasion from the north, building a bridge to carry his huge army over the straits of the Hellespont—now known as the Dardanelles near the northwestern section of Turkey. The first battles of the Persian War went badly for the Greeks, but in 480 BC, the Persian navy was nearly destroyed at the Battle of Salamis, and one year later the Greeks crushed the remainder of

Persian Art and Architecture

The ruins of Darius's Persepolis, as well as his palace at Pasargadae in the Fars province, show archaeologists that the king favored a monumental style of building. His lavish palace was built more than 2,000 years ago in the area that is now southwestern Iran. The palace featured elegant temples and the tomb of Cyrus II, known as the king of kings. Persepolis, the capital of Persia that replaced Pasargadae, was begun in the sixth century BC as a springtime residence of the Persian kings. Situated in a remote and mountainous region, Persepolis remained a safe haven unaffected by invasion until 330 BC, when Alexander the Great sacked the city and burned the Palace of Xerxes.

Various walls, columns, and sculptures, many of which are inscribed, mark the ruins of Persepolis, some of which rest against the Kuh-e Rahmat, or Mountain of Mercy. The stones were laid without mortar and were precision-cut and gray in color. The oldest inscription was carved to mark the words of King Darius: "God protect this country from foe, famine, and falsehood." Still other relief sculptures abound near the site, mostly depicting Persian, Median, and Elamite officials who served the Achaemenid Empire. Notable architecture of the period also includes rock tombs at Naqsh-e-Rostam, which house the remains of the Achaemenian kings—Xerxes, Darius I, Darius II, and Artaxerxes I.

This photograph shows all that remains of the entrance hall of the Gate of Xerxes, once a part of the imposing Palace of Xerxes, located in Persepolis, in present-day Iran. Archaeological evidence has shown that the structure was burned, which matches legends that Alexander the Great deliberately destroyed it in a fire.

the Persian army at the ancient city of Plataea.

This was a bad omen for the future. The balance of power had shifted against the Persians, though it would be many years before the complete fall of the Achaemenid Empire.

2 THE SECOND PERSIAN EMPIRE

After the failure of the Persians to conquer Greece in 479 BC, the Achaemenid Empire began a slow, steady decline. Xerxes was assassinated in 465 BC, and the men who followed him as emperor often did so only by killing their rivals; one of them, Artaxerxes III, killed eighty men in a single day.

Meanwhile, Greek power was gradually increasing. Greek soldiers were already some of the best in the world—even the Persians frequently hired them as mercenaries, a name sometimes given to soldiers hired into foreign service. For most of the hundred years following the Persian War, however, the Greeks fought among themselves. This changed with the rise of Macedonia. Under their king Philip, the Macedonians had adopted both the Greek language and fighting methods. The Macedonians improved those methods until they were able to conquer all of Greece and unite it under Philip's rule in 338 BC. When he was assassinated just two years later, the stage was set for one of the most remarkable military stories in ancient history.

Alexander the Great

Philip's young son Alexander soon proved to be an excellent soldier, and later a great general. After crushing all resistance to Macedonian rule, including destroying the city of Thebes in 335 BC, Alexander was ready to tackle the might of the Persian Empire. He did so not only because of the traditional rivalry between the Greeks and the Persians but also to avenge the earlier Persian invasion of Greece. The wealth of the Persian Empire also made it a tempting target for any would-be conqueror.

The Persian forces vastly outnumbered Alexander's small army. However, the Greek general had several advantages over the Persians. First, his men were the best-trained and disciplined troops in the region. Second, the Persian Empire had been decaying for years, its leadership crumbling from the inside. Alexander knew that he could rely upon many of the Persians turning against their emperor, Darius III. Finally, Alexander himself was a great leader and military commander, qualities that later made him a legend.

By the spring of 334 BC, Alexander's men confronted the Persians for the first time at the Granicus River in Asia Minor. There he routed the emperor's forces and forced the Persians to retreat from the western coastal regions. Alexander and his army followed the Persians, and in 333 BC, he fought with them again, this

time at Issus. During this conflict, Darius himself led the Persians. But Alexander's Macedonians again crushed them, forcing Darius to flee northward. Shortly after, Alexander proclaimed himself the king of Asia.

Alexander then turned south, conquering Phoenicia and Palestine (present-day Lebanon, Israel, and

The mosaic pictured on these pages dates from the first century BC and illustrates Alexander the Great charging Darius as he leads the Persian army in the Battle of Issus in 333 BC. Now housed in the Naples Museum in Italy, the mosaic was originally discovered in Pompeii in the early part of the nineteenth century.

Jordan) and then Egypt itself. In 331 BC, he founded the famous city of Alexandria in Egypt, thereafter a center of learning and culture for hundreds of years.

Later that same year, Alexander returned to Persia, defeated Darius again at Gaugamela, and effectively ended the Persian Empire. Alexander looted the royal city of Susa and then

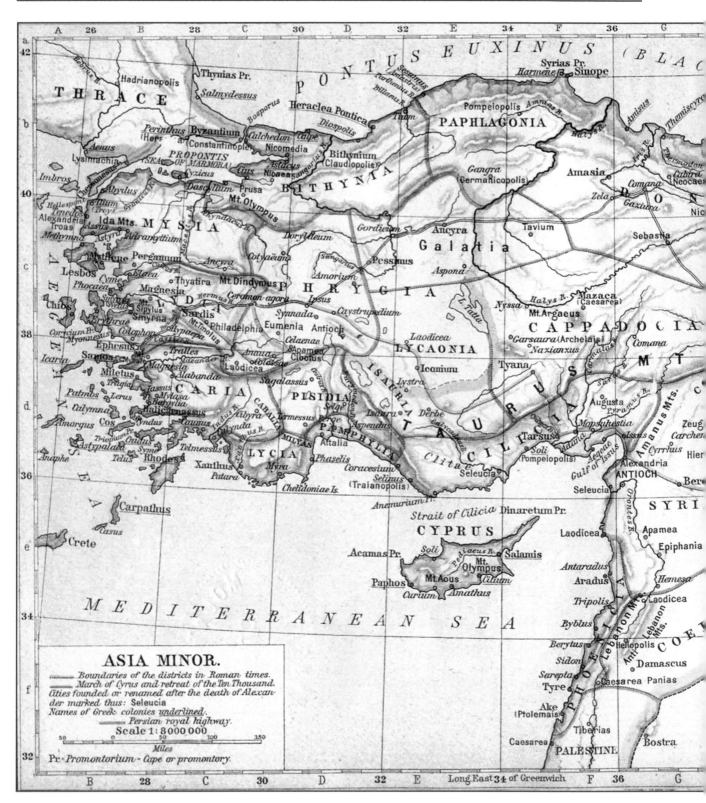

ASIA MINOR.

━━━━━━ Boundaries of the districts in Roman times.
━━━━━━ March of Cyrus and retreat of the Ten Thousand.
Cities founded or renamed after the death of Alexander marked thus: Seleucia
Names of Greek colonies underlined.
━━━━━━ Persian royal highway.
Scale 1 : 8 000 000

Miles

Pr.-Promontorium - Cape or promontory.

William R. Shepherd first printed this historical map of Asia Minor in 1923 in *The Historical Atlas*. The map shows Roman districts in red and territories claimed by Alexander the Great in blue. The official roads of the Persians are depicted in black parallel lines.

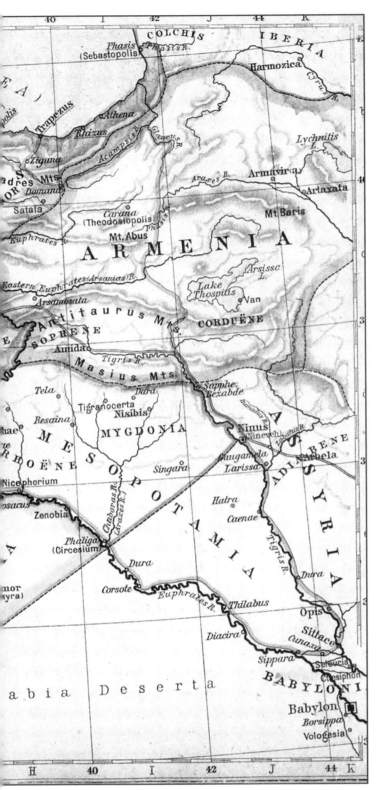

destroyed the capital of Persepolis. When King Darius was murdered by his satraps while fleeing into eastern Iran, Alexander proclaimed himself to be the new emperor.

But Alexander's rule was short-lived. After traveling farther east into India, founding many Macedonian cities on the way, his troops finally refused to go any farther after reaching the Ganges River. He turned back for Macedonia but got only as far as Babylon where, in 323 BC, at the age of thirty-three, Alexander the Great died of what historians believe was malaria.

The Seleucids and the Parthians

Following the death of Alexander the Great, the vast territories of his empire came under the rule of his generals, the most powerful of whom was Seleucus. The generals, who almost immediately fell to squabbling among themselves, fought the so-called War of the Diadochi, and Alexander's vast conquests were never again united under a single leader.

Iran was ruled by the Seleucids for several centuries. Seleucus had gained control of Alexander's conquests in Asia, establishing the Seleucid dynasty. In eastern Iran, however, a revolt was led by a king named Arsaces, ruler of the ancient

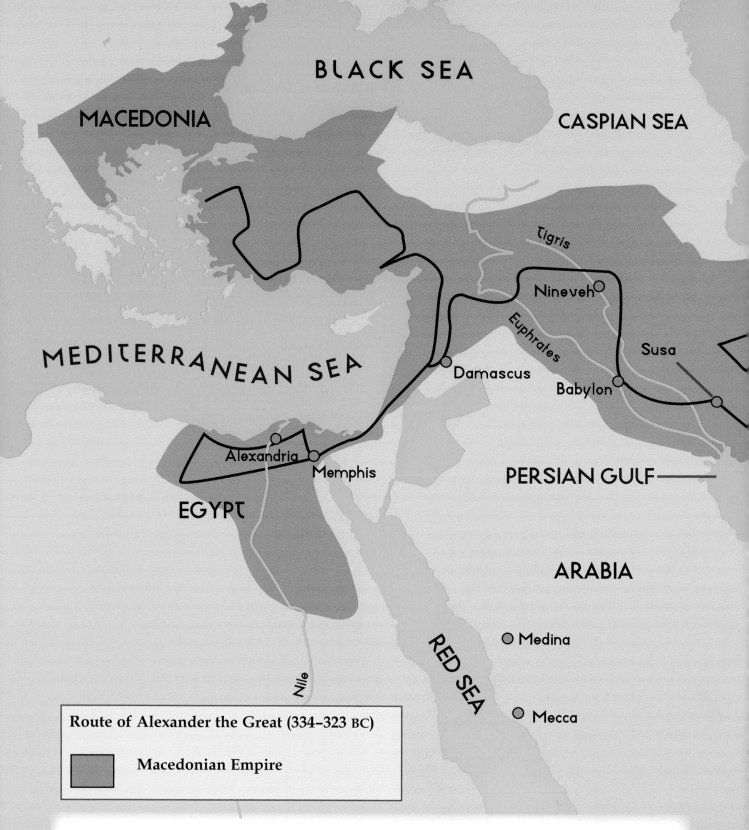

BLACK SEA

MACEDONIA

CASPIAN SEA

Tigris

Nineveh

Susa

MEDITERRANEAN SEA

Damascus

Euphrates

Babylon

Alexandria

PERSIAN GULF

Memphis

EGYPT

ARABIA

○ Medina

RED SEA

Nile

○ Mecca

Route of Alexander the Great (334–323 BC)

Macedonian Empire

During his thirteen years as a celebrated Macedonian ruler, Alexander the Great toppled many cities through-out Asia, claiming them for his empire and renaming them after himself. Never able to consolidate his territory, which before his death stretched from the Mediterranean Sea to India's Indus River, Alexander gave into vices and anger and died unexpectedly in Babylon after being carried into Nebuchadrezzar's palace.

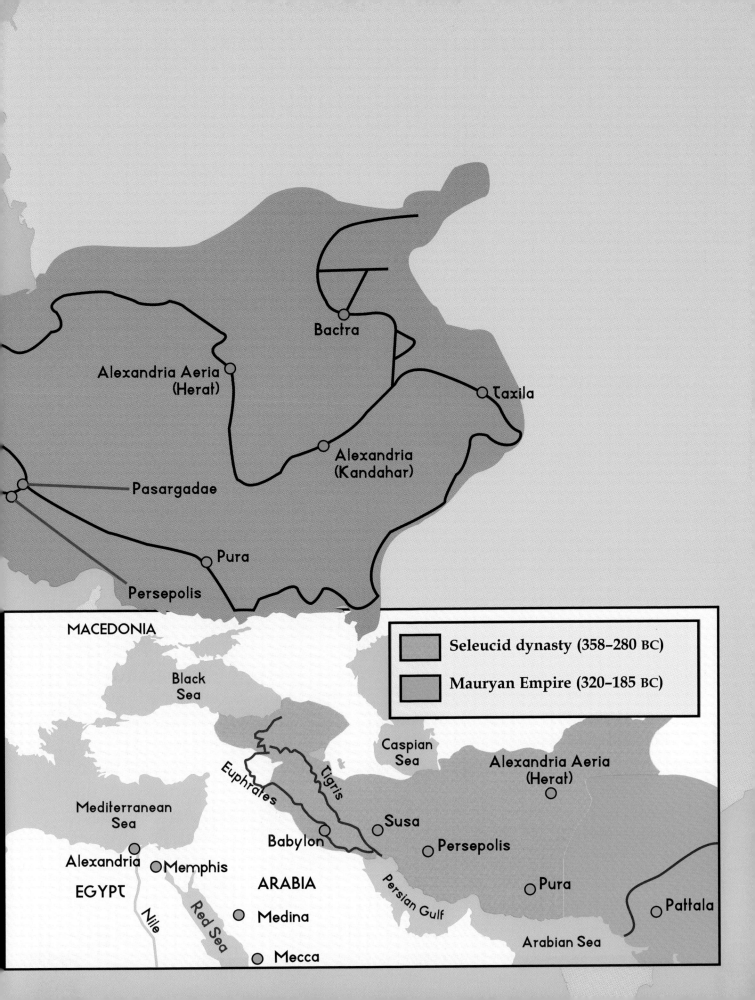

Bactra

Alexandria Aeria
(Herat)

Taxila

Alexandria
(Kandahar)

Pasargadae

Pura

Persepolis

MACEDONIA

Black
Sea

Caspian
Sea

Alexandria Aeria
(Herat)

Euphrates

Tigris

Mediterranean
Sea

Susa

Babylon

Persepolis

Alexandria

Memphis

EGYPT

ARABIA

Pura

Persian Gulf

Medina

Nile

Red Sea

Pattala

Mecca

Arabian Sea

Seleucid dynasty (358–280 BC)

Mauryan Empire (320–185 BC)

Antiochus III, also known as Antiochus the Great, king of Syria (reigned 223–187 BC), ascended to the Seleucid throne as the empire was in decline. Although he attempted to develop the empire further, the Romans repeatedly defeated his armies.

kingdom of Parthia located southeast of the Caspian Sea. His subjects, the Parthians, succeeded in throwing off Seleucid control in 238 BC. Within a century, the Parthians had invaded and reconquered western Iran and Mesopotamia. These conquests brought them into conflict with the mightiest empire in Mediterranean history: Rome.

The Romans had been expanding from central Italy for over a century when they came into conflict with the Parthians. In 53 BC, the Roman leader Crassus led an army against the Parthians and was crushed at the Battle of Carrhae. From that point forward, the two empires were locked in a struggle that would last for hundreds of years.

Little is known about the workings of the Parthian Empire. They spoke their own language, Parthian, but few of their records have survived. Initially, they preserved much of the Hellenistic culture of their Greek conquerors, using Greek as an official language until the first century AD. The Parthian Empire was loosely governed, with noble families having enormous power. This would result in the collapse of Parthian rule and the rise of the Sassanians, yet another Persian dynasty.

The Sassanians

In AD 205, in the province of Fars, the heartland of the old Achaemenid rulers, a revolt against the Parthian leaders developed, led by the commander of the region's troops, Ardashir. In 224, he defeated the last Parthian king, Artabanus V, and laid the formation of the Sassanian dynasty. Ardashir took the title shahanshah, or king of kings, of Iran.

Unlike the Parthians, the Sassanians believed in a strong king and took steps to reestablish his power.

Many of these changes were aimed at winning the loyalty of the subjects by improving their lives. Many new cities were founded, and new irrigation projects were started to help grow larger crops. The Sassanian rulers also tried to make their laws fair and established courts of justice throughout the empire.

The real foundation of Sassanian power, however, was the Zoroastrian religion. This had been the traditional religion of Iran since before the time of Cyrus the Great, but the Persians and Parthians had been tolerant of other forms of worship. The Sassanians, on the other hand, made Zoroastrianism the official religion of Iran.

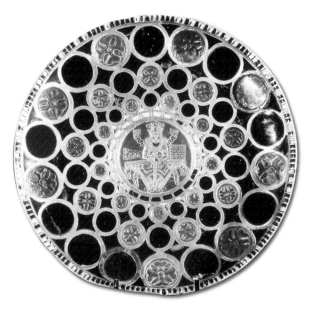

The Sassanians, who ruled Iran from the third century to the seventh century, made enormous contributions to Iranian art and architecture. This crystal and gold dish, like other Sassanian wares, is highly decorated. Sassanian artisans were fond of animal and hunting scenes and repeated patterns.

Zoroastrianism

Founded around 600 BC by the Persian prophet Zoroaster (628–551 BC), also known as Zarathrustra, Zoroastrianism taught that there were two gods—Ahura Mazda, or the "Wise Lord," a good god who had created the universe, and Ahriman, an evil god who opposed him. Zoroastrianism had a wide-ranging influence on religions that developed after it, namely Judaism and Christianity. It also had many followers in the later Roman Empire. The religion survives among the Parsees of India to the present day. Zoroastrianism spread throughout the Achaemenid Empire until the conquests of Alexander the Great conveyed more Hellenistic beliefs.

The Sassanians, like their Parthian predecessors, found themselves constantly engaged with the Roman Empire. In 260, under Ardashir's son Shapur I, they captured the Roman emperor Valerian, a conflict that was later considered one of the most humiliating defeats in Roman history. For the next 200 years, Rome and Persia fought over which empire would control the kingdom of Armenia, a vital region located between the two territories.

The Sassanians had also come into conflict with the Hephtalites, or White Huns, a nomadic people of central Asia, by the late 400s. Kavadh I used their help to regain power after losing the throne to rivals. His successor, Khosrow I, also known as Chosroes (reigned 531–579), managed to finally

Zoroastrianism, its followers now known as Parsees, was the religion of the Persian kings. Parsees maintain small fires in their homes day and night, a ritual that symbolizes life. This Zoroastrian temple is located in Yazd, Iran, an area highly populated by Parsees. About half of the world's Parsees currently live in Iran.

rid the empire of the Hephtalites by allying with another nomadic people, the Turks. After Khosrow's death, the empire was fatally weakened. There was a great discontent among the people with the rule of the emperors, especially among the nobles who led the armies. These feelings led to a revolt by a descendant of Parthian nobles that nearly toppled the Sassanian dynasty.

In 602, the Persians attacked the Byzantine Empire, the eastern half of the old Roman Empire, which continued to rule Greece and the eastern Mediterranean region for centuries after Rome itself fell in 476. They drove far into Byzantine territories, capturing Jerusalem and then Alexandria in Egypt. By 627, however, the Persians were losing territory back to the Byzantines. They would soon come into contact with Islam, a new religious force that was destined to reshape the world.

3 THE COMING OF ISLAM

In 612, Muhammad, a merchant in the Arabian city of Mecca, had a vision. In his vision, the angel Gabriel commanded him to become a prophet for the one true God, Allah. Although he was eventually forced to flee from Mecca for preaching this new religion, within ten years Muhammad would become the most powerful man in the Arabian subcontinent. Over the next four centuries, his followers would conquer vast territories in Africa, the Middle East, Asia, and Europe. Muhammad became known as the Prophet, and the new religion he founded is called Islam. Followers of Islam are known as Muslims.

A monotheistic religion rooted in both Judaism and Christianity, Islam preaches the worship of only one God, who created the world and will judge all human beings at the end of time. Like Christianity, Islam teaches that there is a paradise to which people who have lived good lives will ascend, and there is a hell for evildoers. Islam exploded into the Middle East and spread even more rapidly than Christianity had less than six centuries before. Islam became the religion of Persians, and Arabic became the official language of Iran. Even today, Persians use a modified version of the Arabic script.

Part of the reason that Islam rose so quickly was because of the military skill of the Arabs. For centuries, the nomadic tribes of Arabia had been in a state of near constant conflict, frequently raiding each other for goods and livestock. But now, united behind Muhammad and his caliphs, or successors, they effortlessly swept ancient empires, conquering everything in their path. After Muhammad's death in 632, Abu Bakr became his successor, or the first Islamic caliph.

By the 630s, the Arabs under Bakr's leadership had come into direct conflict with the Sassanians. In 637, the Arabs won all of Mesopotamia. By 642, they had crushed the last Sassanian army and were in full control of western Iran. Eastern Iran, never very loyal to the Sassanians, was fully in the hands of the Arabs by 653. At first the Muslim invaders allowed the free practice of outside religions, but that would soon change.

The introduction of Islam to the region now known as Iran caused profound change. The old Zoroastrian religion was swept away and replaced by the Islamic religion of the conquerors. At the same time, contact with Iran changed Islam. Exposure to the ancient Persian culture gave the faith a greater philosophical depth. Persian art and poetry greatly enriched Islam's cultural heritage. Both Iran and Islam were changed by the conquest, each becoming more culturally enriched.

Alexandria O

EGYPT

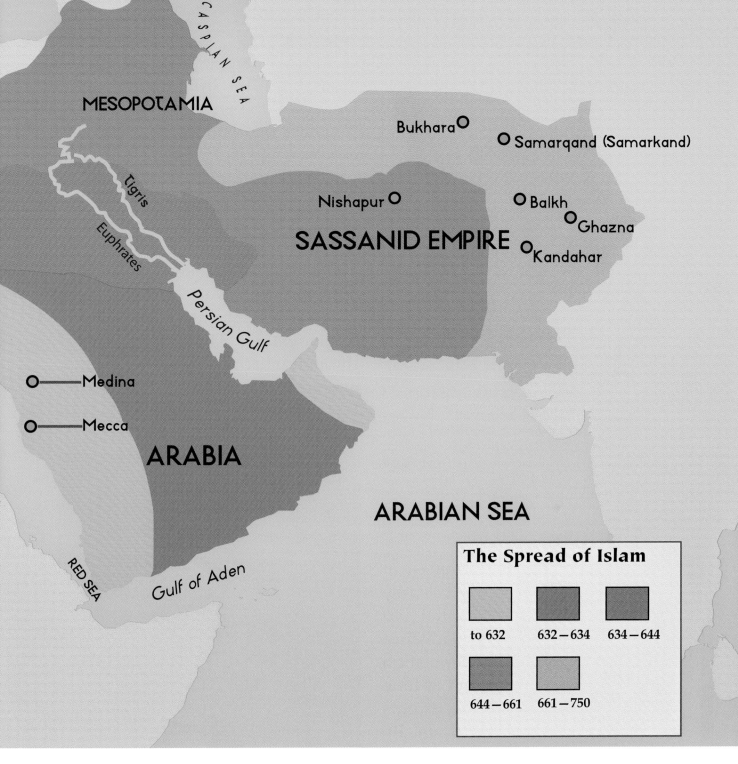

The Islamic faith spread rapidly, as shown on this map, after the death of its prophet, Muhammad, in AD 632. Not merely a faith to its Muslim followers, Islam, a word meaning "submission," then represented a total way of life, just as it does today. Spread by Muslim armies in less than two decades, Islam's message reached Syria (AD 635), Iraq (AD 637), Palestine (AD 640), Egypt (AD 642), and the entire Persian Empire (AD 650). Later, the faith would continue to find followers through the travels of Muslim merchants and Sufis (mystics). Today, Islam remains one of the world's most widely followed religions. The Mosque of Imam (left), located in Isfahan, Iran, was built under the leadership of Safavid-era leader Shah Abbas I (reigned 1587–1629), who made the city the capital of Persia in 1598. Completed over a period of eighteen years, the Mosque of Imam is a splendid example of Persian architecture and design.

This Persian manuscript page from AD 1237 illustrates a procession marking the end of Ramadan, the traditional month of daylight fasting that marks the ninth month in the Muslim lunar calendar. The original manuscript is now housed in the Bibliothèque Nationale in Paris.

The Seljuks

For 400 years after the conquest of Iran by the Arabs, Iran was ruled by caliphs from their capital in Baghdad, the present-day capital of Iraq. However, the Arab population of Iran was never large, and as time went by, many Iranian customs dominated over those of Islam. By the 900s, Persian was being revived as the national language of Iran, and translations of major Arabic works were commonplace.

Soon, however, a new group would arrive to change the face of Iran. These people were the Turks, nomadic tribes from central Asia. Drawn by the wealth of the Islamic caliphate, they had taken jobs as mercenaries and soldiers, becoming a powerful military force for the caliphs. Other Turks, called Turkomans, had voluntarily converted to Islam and were founding their own systems of government. One of these self-governed groups, the Seljuks, moved south into present-day Afghanistan. They then swept through what is now known as Iran and into Mesopotamia, conquering Baghdad in 1055. By 1071, the Seljuks

The remains of a twelfth-century Seljuk caravansary, or caravan station, along a major trade route of the Silk Road. The Silk Road was a series of ancient highways that linked present-day Europe to China.

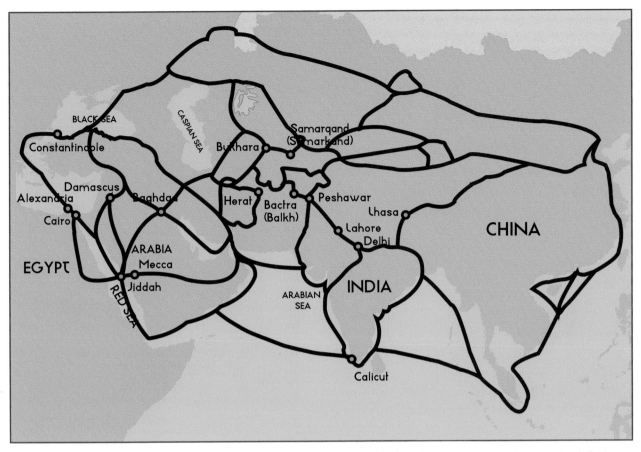

The Silk Road, a 5,000-mile (8,047-kilometer) trade route over land and sea was somewhat repaired during the Seljuk Empire and more completely restored during the Mongol Empire. The goal of both peoples was to make the trade routes safer for traveling. The Seljuks, in fact, were the first people to build a network of rest houses along the Silk Road, and called the most luxurious of those shelters caravanserai. The distance between the caravanserai was calculated on the basis of travel time by hours, usually about every ninth hour, so that shelter could be found at the end of an average day of camel riding.

had defeated the Byzantine Empire at Manzikert. The Seljuks believed in a strong central governing system, one that focused on a central leader. This victory at Manzikert exposed medieval Anatolia, now in present-day Turkey, to further Turkic conquest and eventually brought them into conflict with Christian crusaders from western Europe.

Although the Seljuk Empire declined after the murder of the powerful Iranian vizier, or political adviser, Nizam al-Mulk in 1092, Iran enjoyed an era of increased cultural expression. Driven by advancements in the arts and in architecture that would later have a valuable impact on its culture, the main branch of the Seljuk sultanate helped Iranian culture reach an elevated distinction.

Retaining much of their nomadic culture, the Seljuks were not able to

Omar Khayyam

Omar Khayyam (1048–1131), known almost exclusively in the West as a Persian poet, was also a gifted scholar, mathematician, and astronomer. Born in Naishapur, a medieval Persian city, shortly before the Seljuk conflict, Khayyam was responsible for many achievements in scientific learning. He compiled astronomical tables, contributed to reforming the calendar to reflect a 365-day year, and wrote several informative books about mathematics, including *Problems of Arithmetic* and *Treatise on Demonstration of Problems in Algebra*. His most famous book of poetry, *The Rubáiyát*, was translated and compiled by an Englishman named Edward Fitzgerald in 1859. Even today, it remains one of the most widely read works of Eastern literature in the world.

This twentieth-century illustration by Gilbert James depicts a scene from the *Rubáiyát* of Omar Khayyam, a book of poetry well known throughout the world.

administer a large empire, and individual military commanders frequently operated as independent rulers. The continued raiding and migration by other Turkic tribes into their territory further weakened the Seljuk government. By 1157, these tribes had overrun much of the empire. But future disasters were awaiting Iran. Genghis Khan, the most powerful warlord since Alexander the Great, was approaching from the north. And soon, centuries of Iranian and Islamic culture would be dramatically and brutally silenced at the hand of Mongol hordes.

4 MONGOL INVASIONS

Even Islam could not withstand the devastation that was about to descend upon it from China in the north. Mongol hordes, under the leadership of Genghis Khan, terrorized Persia and its people, killing populations of entire regions.

Genghis Khan

Temüjin, known later as Genghis (Chinggis) Khan (1162–1227), rose from obscurity to become the leader of nomadic tribes throughout the region known as Mongolia. Using the united might of the greatest horsemen in the world, he turned his Mongol armies against China, overrunning it by 1215. He then turned westward, invading present-day Russia and central Asia.

At the time, the Mongol armies were the most effective military in the world. They were masters at spreading terror among their rivals. Their basic method of attack was to encircle their enemies and then assault them with deadly archers. Many times they were deceptive and pretended to retreat in order to lure their enemies into a trap.

In 1219, the Mongols arrived in Persia, an invasion spawned in response to the murder of one of their ambassadors. For the next four years, they spread destruction throughout the region, nearly destroying

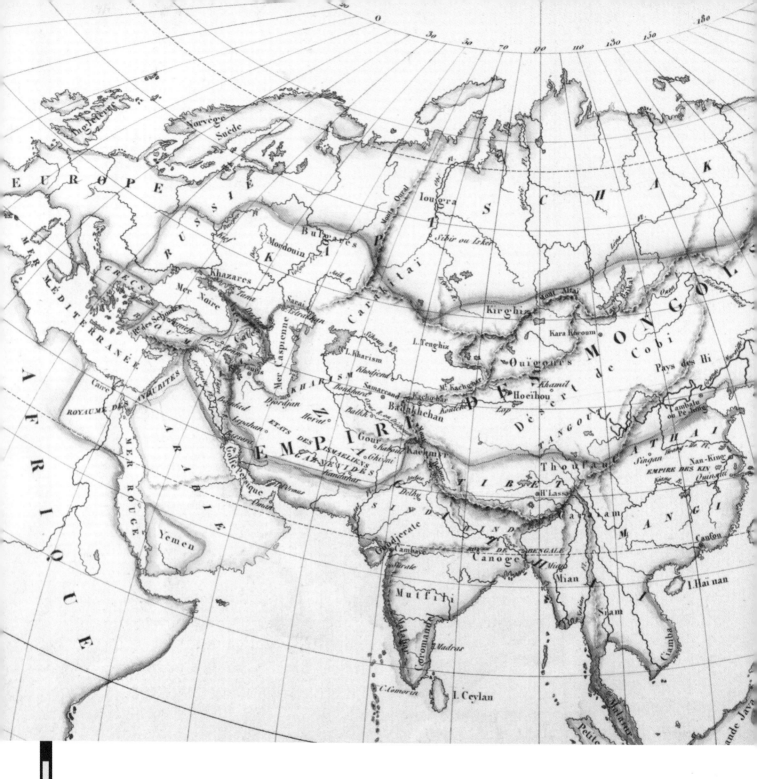

The map pictured here, a nineteenth-century engraving, depicts the Mongol Empire at its height (approximately AD 1300), stretching from present-day Beijing, China, to Istanbul, Turkey. Mongol forces completely overtook the Persian Empire, except for a few small areas that resisted its power. At first led by Genghis Khan, shown in this detail of a Chinese silk painting *(right)*, the Mongol hordes killed thousands and destroyed cities in their wake. As a result, important Persian artifacts and architecture were lost forever. It wasn't until the sixteenth century, when the Safavid dynasty gained power, that Persia could truly dominate the region once more. This period of growth and artistic expression later became known as the Third Persian Empire (1502–1722).

the beautiful and ancient cities of Merv, Balkh, and Naishapur.

By 1255, approximately twenty-eight years after the death of Genghis Khan, the Mongols returned. This time their conquest of the region was permanent. They swept through Persia into Mesopotamia, capturing Baghdad and ending the rule of the caliphs. The Mongol territory now included present-day Iran, Iraq, and Turkey, as well as the Caucasus region. Genghis Khan's grandson, Hülegü, who led the conquest, established a new government, the Ilkhanate. For the next 300 years, his descendants ruled Iran.

At first, the Mongol domination of Iran was destructive. Mongol administrators cruelly taxed the population, and the upkeep of the delicate system vital to growing food was neglected. The Mongols were also hostile toward Islam and tried to suppress the religion throughout the region.

However, under Ghazan Khan, who ruled from 1295 to 1304, this suppression of religion ceased. Ghazan converted to Islam under the influence of his Iranian vizier, Rashid-al-Din, and tried to reform the taxation system.

Ghazan's reforms came too late, however. In 1335, the last Mongol ruler, Abu Said, died, and no successor could be agreed upon. Present-day Iran again disintegrated into warring tribal regions.

As brutal as their leadership was, the Mongols did not destroy Iranian culture. Indeed, many great works of

Miniature Painting

Painting in miniature flourished during the Mongol period from the thirteenth to sixteenth centuries. Mongolian rulers, migrating south from China, popularized the style of illustrative painting, which, incidentally, coincided with the introduction of paper to Persia in 753. Both poetry and art matured in Shiraz, the capital of Fars. Decorative Arabic writing was further influenced by eloquent Chinese calligraphy, and poetic themes were introduced as narrative visual plots in paintings. Three of the most influential schools of miniature painting were Shiraz, Tabriz, and Herat.

This Islamic miniature painting of Muslims praying in a mosque is indicative of the types of miniatures found in Iran that date as far back as the thirteenth century. Now famous throughout the world, Persian miniature paintings are highly sought after works of art that usually depict scenes from daily life, such as courting couples, hunting, and polo matches. Modern Iranian artisans have kept up the tradition of painting in miniature, many working in Isfahan.

literature and art came out of this period. The Persian-Islamic culture of Iran survived and flourished, even during a period of Mongol conquest. Still, nearly two centuries would pass before a truly united Iran would emerge.

Timur

Although he spoke Turkish, Timur (1336–1405) was a descendant of the Mongol conquerors of Iran. He was also known as Tamerlane or Timur the Lame because he had been wounded in battle and walked with a limp. Timur rose from obscurity to become one of history's great conquerors. Unlike his model, Genghis Khan, however, Timur had no greater ambition of creating a permanent empire; his conquests proved nothing except his military leadership.

Timur's life was spent in constant military conflict. He first fought against the tribes of central Asia,

The sixteenth-century Persian manuscript page reproduced on this page illustrates Timur, a medieval conqueror who claimed to be a descendant of Genghis Khan. Because he was not directly linked to the Mongols, however, he chose to influence his subjects by showing a great deal of religious piety toward Islam and instead took the title of emir. During his long lifetime, Timur conquered Persia (Iran), Azerbaijan, Armenia, Georgia, northern Iraq, Syria, and nearly all of Asia Minor and northern India.

then in the conquest of Iran (1387), and finally in the invasion and ultimate destruction of the last of the Mongol states in central Asia, the Golden Horde. He conquered Mesopotamia and invaded India, conquering the sultanate of Delhi in 1398. His final years were spent fighting the Ottoman Turks.

Timur was by far the cruelest of the Mongol rulers. He destroyed cities and had the inhabitants of entire regions killed. He left a trail of death and destruction across central Asia and the Middle East. At the same time he supported great works of art and architecture in his homeland of Samarkand.

His successors, the Timurids, however, brought a period of peace and enlightenment back to Iran. The Timurids made Herat their capital, and it became a beautiful city of mosques and monuments. A member of their line also founded the Mughal dynasty in India.

Unfortunately, the reign of the Timurids was brief. In 1469, Turkoman invaders conquered the area that is now western Iran, and in 1507, Uzbek Turks from central Asia conquered remaining Timurid territory.

5 THE THIRD PERSIAN EMPIRE

Uniting Persia after the Mongol invasions of the prior years was a demanding undertaking. The Safavids, a successful Persian military and political dynasty, are notable for laying the cultural and political basis of modern Iran.

The Safavids

In 1395, Shaykh Safi ad Din founded a religious order in central Asia that became known as the Safavids. Originally they were merely one of many Sufi orders in the region, followers of a mystical version of Islam. Within fifty years, however, the Safavids had changed into a warrior order, dedicated to fighting enemies of the faith and espousing Shiism.

The Shiites are one of the two major branches of Islam; the other is called Sunni

This sixteenth-century map of Persia, named "The Kingdom of Persia" or "The Empire of the Sophies," dates from 1580 and was included in the first edition of Dutch cartographer Abraham Ortelius's *Theatrum Orbis Terrarum*, the first modern atlas. Known today for his accuracy and detail, Ortelius commonly used both his own maps and those of other cartographers to whom he attributed authorship. After Ortelius's death, more than forty editions of his atlas were printed from 1570 to 1624, including translations from Dutch into Latin, German, Spanish, French, Italian, and English.

Septentrio.

pars

Caracus

Pagansa

Eilach
Ocerra

Teras
Sabat

Sosechi
Samahin
Benohes
Chind sm fruhmi

Tachamia
Auacton
Vargut

Xibuar
Iarchen

Calba
Cotan
Tom

Ciarcian
Lop.

Chesel olim laxartes
Cant
Siminan
Giend
Teras
Sebgu

Agrian fan
Feras

ASRVSEN.
Ispanichics
Reuen
Ltairan

SAFANIAN.
Tinchit

Iarchen
Mogalachsu

Acsu

ZAGATAI Tart:
Mora
Madrandan
Lachozibet
Salu
Ches
Beighebt

Samarchan d magni
Tamberlanis re
Meryilan
Tascan

SAMARCHAND
SIM.

Terment
Sachi
Anachon

Vachirat lan
Velgirt
Achsiges

CIARCIAN.
Labor
Chuche

OCRAGE
Lere
Carasian
Zahaspa
Abiarni olim
Oxus fl.
Derisian
Maru
Corus
Sarachiuch
Corsuni
Buccara
Chiarga
Amu lacus
Chesini
Tauais
Bichend
Diamuch
Coman

SVISITVR gum
Naseph
Erbigien

Merglan

SACHI.
Cheresian
Giorgi ane
Samacl sir
Cax
Sermengan
Danran

TACALISTAN
L sarest
Veluuling

TARTAR
SIVE IM
RII MAG
CHAMI

BVCCARA.
Babacanter lacus
Abia fl.
Chiarachar
Bigul
Farad

Espunuches
GIECVM.
I Aigias

ISTIGIAS.
Ariandar
Cheng

R ugi siri sith desertum
Nimer don BAT.
Chescun
Anducaton
Girgian
Cheche

IESEL
BAS.
Germop

Bigul desertum
Varcana

CHARASSAN
Busdachsan
Oborgit fl.
Serbercho

BEDANE
Badagilan
BALCH

Hie turchini gemme reperi untur
Sebsar
Cheli dar
Sesara
Derbel
Giang
Calegert

IESE
LBAS.
Indion
Sifelech M.
Burgit M.

Werber
Panjan
Arylan

Termes
Gerin

Escal cand
Dalanguer M.

MESAT
Tazum
Ergert
Mazan
Cusa
Turis Saturgei
Chedul teran
Burgian
Caussiend
Balcon fl.
Balch
Tochte
Bagsiur
Endras

SABLESTAN.

Abile forts

CAPACOP.
Langer
Pacnalen
Jugan
Digitan
Caris
Schenon
Besneri
Corho
BAICHIS
Pulimato fl.
Lacus
Burgian
Calchastan M.

Serent
Basoabai
Turbeh
Chiutessur
Tebezulichi
COR
Busnana
Cosana
Cain
Sadami
Sercha
Coibocaran
Montes

CABVL.

GVADEL
Bidleng
Rouee
Cabis
MA
Serent
Tachisandan Mons
Rachari
Canal
Lebesmi sma
Lire

SI GISTAN.
Casallatia
Asian

Multan
Suminqt
Sind

Benpir
Sostan
Bagian
Malein

INDIA
GANGE
DOS

Desertum Lut.
CIRCAN.
Cobinan
Daragi
Bulfer
Gesf
Timochan
Sapurjan
Indu

Lobaran
Machlu naua

Tachisandam mons
Chichme ran
Biguri
Eugan
Raitanbur

GVZARATE.

ERACHAIAN
Ardauar
Dulcinda
Pasir
MACRAN.
Macran
Chindu
Albirun
Cafsar
Sidusfan
Amodaban

PERSICI
SIVE SOPHO
RVM REGNI
TYPVS.

Ponta Arestinga

MARE INDICVM, ol. MA
RE RVBRVM.

Meridies.

Islam. The Shiites believe that only members of Muhammad's family can succeed him as the leaders of the Islamic community. The largest grouping of Shiites, to which the Safavids belonged, are called Twelver Shiites, since they believe that there were twelve successors to Muhammad; the twelfth and last has gone into hiding and will return one day as the Mahdi, or the Islamic messiah.

Beginning in 1500, the Safavids began a conquest of the region that now encompasses Iran, sweeping away the various Turkic ruling tribes. By 1510, they had conquered most of the region as well as Mesopotamia. However, their conquests brought them into conflict

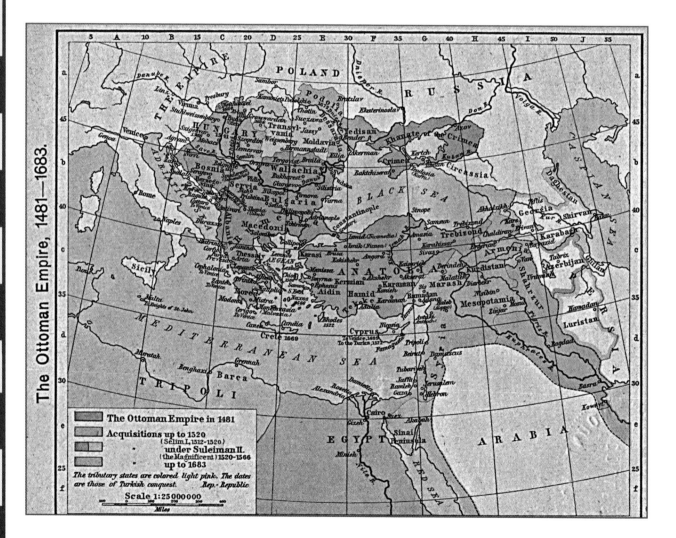

Though the Safavids attempted to threaten the Muslim Ottoman Empire in 1514, they would not gain territory until 1598 under Shah Abbas I (1571–1629). By that time, the Ottomans had expanded their empire into Europe and the Mediterranean under Suleiman the Magnificent (1494–1566), as shown on this map. The Safavids' late sixteenth-century conquest of Ottoman land included present-day Azerbaijan and Armenia.

with the Uzbeks in the east and the Ottoman Turks in the west.

In 1514, at the Battle of Chaldiran, Ottoman Turks, who had superior troops armed with gunpowder weapons, defeated the Safavid forces. The conflict caused the Safavids to lose control of Mesopotamia; meanwhile, the struggles against the Uzbeks prevented expansion farther east. The Safavid Empire would be restricted to the area of modern Iran.

One of the most important consequences of the Safavids' rule in Iran was the establishment of Shiite Islam as the dominant form of religion. This change made Iran unique among its neighbors, most of which practiced Sunni Islam and allowed nominal allegiance to the caliphate located in Baghdad, and later in Istanbul. This was one reason that both the Ottomans and Uzbeks were enemies of the Safavids. Also, Shiism gives great power to the clerics, who have the responsibility of interpreting Islamic law, unlike Sunni Islam, which has no religious clergy. This would have enormous influence on the future of modern Iran.

Under the rule of Abbas I, who reigned from 1587 to 1629, the Safavids reached their greatest height. His capital, Isfahan, became one of the most beautiful cities in the world. His reign also saw the arrival of Europeans into the Persian Gulf

Safavid-era Shah Abbas I employed successful domestic policies and recaptured Tabriz, a city held by the Turks for eighteen years. He also gained control over the important trading base of Hormuz, which improved the economy of the empire. His reign made possible a more unified Persian culture with a national language (Farsi).

and Iran's first direct contact with western Europe.

The Safavids fell into decline after the reign of Abbas I. The rulers of the empire became increasingly corrupt, and the army was neglected. In 1722, Afghan tribesmen conquered Isfahan, effectively ending the Safavid Empire.

A tribal chief who crowned himself Nadir Shah (sometimes called "the Persian Napoleon") ruled most of Iran from 1736 until his assassination in

Isfahan

Isfahan, a medieval Persian city founded by Abbas I and made the capital of Persia in 1598, reached its height in the seventeenth century. Under Abbas, Isfahan was completely rebuilt with oversized avenues, magnificent gardens, and a splendid royal palace. Though its splendor lasted a little more than 100 years, it was once among the most artistic and well-respected cities in the entire Islamic world. As a capital, Isfahan was centrally located and boasted an important trading center. The city was ultimately known for its contributions to religion, culture, and government. Isfahan itself is peppered with historic monuments, mosques, and bridges, and is surrounded by the Zayandeh-Rud. One of its most famous sites is the Imam Square, or Royal Square, which was once the center of the Safavid dynasty and was used for polo games and large gatherings. Isfahan is also famous for the Masjed-e-Jomeh, or the Friday Mosque. Given that the city has had such an illustrious past, it is not surprising that a rhythmic sixteenth-century phrase is often linked to its history. *Isfahan nesf-eh jahan*, loosely translated, means "Isfahan is half of the world." Today, Isfahan proudly hosts many tourists who wander its majestic bridges, gardens, shops, and teahouses rich in history.

Isfahan, as shown in this aerial photograph, shows just some of its Safavid-era splendor. The Royal Square and Friday Mosque, the remains of which are pictured here, were constructed during the reign of Shah Abbas I.

1747. He sacked Delhi in India in 1738 and returned with the Koh-i-noor diamond and the fabulous Peacock Throne, encrusted with precious jewels. Later, the opulent throne became a symbol of the Iranian shahs. After Nadir Shah's death, Iran fell into a period of civil war between rival factions and was without a unified government until 1795.

6 THE SHAHS

Iran's strategic location in Asia made it a prime target for invasion throughout the centuries. This became especially evident in the nineteenth century during the Qajar dynasty, when Iran became vulnerable to European outsiders, as well as to its Russian neighbors to the north.

The Qajars

Following the death of Nadir Shah, Iran fell into a period of struggle between two rival factions, the Zands and Qajars. It was a time of constant rebellions and civil wars. Finally, Aga Muhammed Shah emerged victorious, establishing the new Qajar dynasty in 1796, which governed Iran poorly for the next 130 years.

During the reign of the Qajars, Iran continued to lose power and territory to the European powers that were now moving into the region. Although they never became a colony of one of the European nations, the power of the once dominant empire continued to decline.

The main opponent of Qajar Iran was Russia. Once a less-prominent European nation, Russia had thrived under the leadership of Peter the Great (reigned 1682–1725) and Catherine the Great (reigned 1762–1796) and was now actively expanding its influence in central Asia. Iran was also

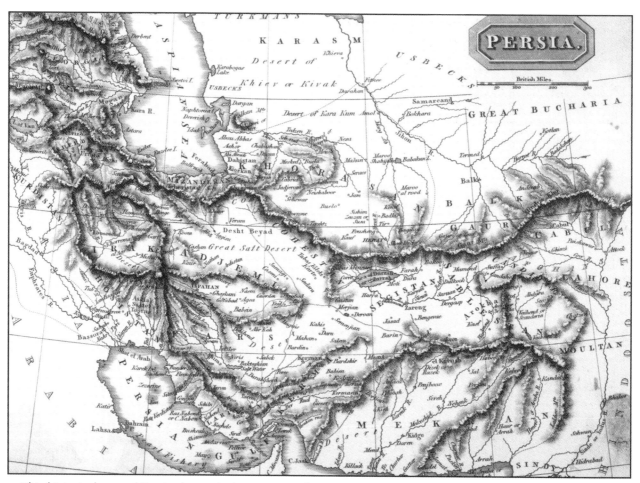

This historical map of Persia shows the importance of its territory for Britain and Russia. By the eighteenth century, the Russians wanted access to the Persian Gulf and India, which was heavily traveled by British traders. Britain wanted to control southern Persia to help protect access to India and its profitable trade routes. Before long, both countries had occupied sections of the Persian Empire for these purposes, and, collectively, they began to deplete its natural resources.

involved in conflicts with the British, who wanted to defend their territory in India at all costs and to secure the sea route from India to the Gulf of Aden.

Russia gradually absorbed more and more of the Qajar territories, annexing Georgia in 1801 and the Caucasus regions in 1828. By 1884, Russia had taken the region of Merv in northern Iran. The British eventually dominated southern Iran from their bases in the Persian

Gulf and in India. After the defeat of Iran in the 1856–1857 Anglo-Persian War, the Qajar government began to negotiate a series of concessions. These were agreements that gave countries or companies exclusive access to the resources of Iran. The concessions were sold for a fraction of what they were worth. Qajar rulers lived in luxury at the high cost of their nation's suffering.

Dissent within Iran led to a religious revival. Bahaism, a faith combining Christian and Muslim ideologies, was born following the ill-fated Babi revolt in 1844 and was ruthlessly suppressed by the government. The Shiite clergy, however, were successful in resisting the government. In 1890, they organized protests against the British monopoly on tobacco in Iran, forcing it to be ended. Increasing protests led to the granting of a constitution, with an elected parliament, the Majlis, in 1906. When the Qajars tried to suppress the constitution in 1909, a popular revolt forced the shah, or king, to resign; he returned to power, however, in 1911, through the support of Russian troops.

During World War I (1914–1918), both the Russians and the British occupied Iran. This occupation caused great humiliation for most Iranians, as the final fall of the Qajars neared. By 1921, a colonel in the Iranian army, Reza Khan, led a coup against the

This contemporary painting entitled "A Young Qajar Prince and his Entourage" was painted by Abu'l Hasan to illustrate the leaders of a transitional period in Iranian history between 1796 and 1925. Known as the Qajar Period, it was a time when eighteenth-century Iranian rulers helped create a modern Iranian state after a period of weakness and national division. Although the Qajars were poor reformers, the century of new ideas eventually led to a later period of revolution and a centralized government under the Pahlavi shahs.

government and proclaimed martial law. The era of the Qajars was over, and the era of the Pahlavi dynasty was about to begin.

The Reign of Reza Shah

Born in 1877, the man who would become the first modern ruler of Iran was the son of an army officer. While still known as Reza Khan, he entered the elite Cossack Brigade, a Russian-trained military unit that served the Qajar monarchs. Like many Iranians, Reza Khan grew dissatisfied with the way the Qajars were governing the country. He disliked the occupation of Iran during World War I and felt deeply humiliated by the treaty the British tried to impose on the nation after the war. These feelings of dissent motivated Reza Khan to move against the government. In 1921, he seized power and proclaimed martial law in Iran.

At first, Reza Khan did little to change the structure of Iran. The Qajar shah, Ahmad Shah, remained on the Iranian throne. He appointed Reza Khan as the minister of war, and, in 1923, he became the prime minister before he left for Europe. In 1925, the parliament voted to remove Ahmad Shah and named Reza Khan the new shah of Iran. He was then known as Reza Shah Pahlavi.

Progress and Reform

Reza Shah did much to modernize Iran. He built the Trans-Iranian railroad, imposed a code of law for the country, and supported the education and emancipation of women. He also tried to break much of the Soviet and British influence on the nation. Yet Reza Shah was also an absolute ruler. He viciously crushed the power of the tribal chiefs and did little to improve the country's agricultural needs.

This map of Iran during its phase of outside control by Britain and Russia (right) shows areas of control by both countries during and after World War I. While some areas were totally controlled by British forces, others were only occupied by British and Russian troops. Reza Shah Pahlavi (above) is fondly remembered as an Iranian reform shah who fought for women's rights and increased literacy, and who made efforts to mold Iran into a modernized, secular state. By 1941, Reza Shah was forced into exile for his efforts and succeeded by his son, Muhammad Reza Pahlavi, who led Iran until 1979.

BLACK SEA

CASPIAN SEA

Persian Gulf

RED SEA

ARABIAN SEA

Gulf of Aden

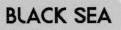 Iranian Territory under British control
during World War I (1914–1918)

POST-WORLD WAR I ZONE OF INFLUENCE

Britain   Russia

The outbreak of World War II signaled the end of Reza Shah's power. Reza Shah's support of the Germans led both Britain and the Soviet Union to invade Iran, and Reza Shah was forced to abdicate. The British declared his son, Muhammad Reza Pahlavi, the new shah, and Reza Shah went into exile. In 1943, Britain, Russia, and the United States accepted Iran as an independent nation, signing the Tehran Declaration.

The Constitutional Revolution

Following the abdication of Reza Shah, Iran once more was under the domination of foreign governments. Yet without Reza Shah's absolute control, however, the Majlis enjoyed a brief period of power in Iran. Steps were taken not only to modernize Iran but also to make it more independent.

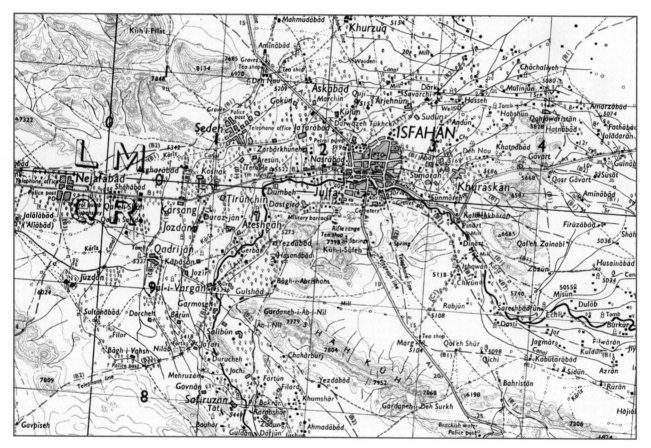

This historic map of Isfahan (above) was compiled and reproduced by the India Field Survey Company in January 1943 and reprinted by the U.S. Army Map Service in July of the same year. The U.S. Central Intelligence Agency (CIA) map (right) shows the approximated populations of people living in the Persian Gulf region in the 1980s. By today's statistics, the approximate populations in the same region are as follows: Sixty-six million people living in Iran, twenty-three million living in Iraq, two million living in Kuwait, twenty-four million living in Saudi Arabia, three million living in Oman, and four million living in the United Arab Emirates.

Dehlorán

Dezfúl

Shūshtar

Al 'Amárah

Dasht-e Āzádegán

Masjed-e Soleymán

Al Qurnah
phrates

IRA

Aḥvāz

Haft Gel

Shahr-e Kord

Zarrin Shahr

EŞFAHĀN

Na'in

Shahreẓā

Ābādeh

Zagros Mountains

Rūd-e Dez

Rūd-e Kārūn

Āghā Jārī

Behbahán

Yásúj

Deh Bid

IRAN

Hawr al Hammār

AL BAŞRAH

Khorramshahr

Shatt al Arab

Ābādán

Bandar-e Khomeynī

Umm Qaṣr

Al Fāw

KUWAIT

Būbiyán

Bandar-e Deylam

Ganáveh

Khárk

Rūd-e Mand

Kuwait

Minā' 'Abd Allāh

Minā' Su'ūd

Būshehr

Kázerún

Shīráz

Sīrjān

Ra's al Khafjī

Firúzábád

Fasā

Jahrom

Gahkom

yat al 'Ulyá

Manīfah

Abū 'Alī

Deyyer

Lár

Bandar-e 'Abbās

Al Jubayl

Bandar-e Moqám

Láván

Qeshm

Strait of Hormuz

Ḥanīdh

Al Qaṭīf

Ras Tanura

Persian Gulf

Kish

Bandar-e Lengeh

ahnā'

SAUDI

Khuraşş

Ad Dammām

Dhahran   Al Khubar

Manama

BAHRAIN

Al Khuwayr

Ḥawār

QATAR

Dukhān

Doha

Sirrī

Tunbs

Abū Mūsá

Ash Sha'm

Ra's al Khaymah

Umm al Qawayn

OMAN
admin.

Ḥiṣn Dibā

Al Hufūf

Musay'īd

in dispute

Dās

Dubayy

Minā' Jabal 'Alī

Al Fujayrah

ADH

Al Şalwā

Şir Banī Yás

Abu Dhabi

Shinâş

ARABIA

As Sulaymānīyah

Ḥaraḍ

Sabkhat Maṭṭī

Al Ruways

UNITED

Bū Ḥasá

ARAB

EMIRATES

Al 'Ayn

no defined boundary

'Arádah

no defined boundary

Al 'Ubaylah

Jibāl

Island names and boundary representation

A major change in the politics of the region came in December 1941 when the United States entered World War II. American troops were stationed in Iran, and the growing American interest in the country was used to break the hold of both the British and the Soviets over Iran. Although it became Iran's most important ally after World War II, the United States ultimately assisted in destroying the democratic reforms established during this period.

The growing need for oil by the United States and the European nations also made Iran vital. Subsequently, the struggle over the control of Iran's oil industry would lead to a major international crisis in the 1950s and after.

Opposition Parties

By 1946, Iran, with the backing of the United States, forced the Soviets to withdraw. After a period of turmoil during which several rebellions were crushed by the Iranian army, the shah's victories made him more popular. In 1949, he called for the creation of a senate, half of whose members would be appointed by him. By doing so, he hoped to curb the growing power of the Majlis. Opposition to the shah was centered in three parties: the Tudeh, or Communist party; the Fedaiyan-I Islam, a conservative party

of Islamic fundamentalists; and the National Front, a liberal and secular, or non-religious, party. The leader of the National Front, Mohammed Mossadeq, became prime minister in 1951.

Mossadeq's first major action was to nationalize, or take over, the powerful Anglo-Iranian Oil Company. Founded in 1909, this British company effectively had total control of all of Iran's oil exports and profits. Angry at this move, the British broke off relations with Iran. Rather than using military force, the British imposed economic sanctions, such as boycotting the import of Iranian products. Also, none of the British employees of the Anglo-Iranian Oil Company remained employed with the new National Iranian Oil Company, which was a major setback for the business.

Mossadeq's actions made him a hero in Iran. He used his popularity to assume greater control of the government. When he no longer had control over the Majlis, he illegally called for new elections in 1953. After this development, the American and British governments decided to overthrow Mossadeq. Aware of the plot against him, Mossadeq allied with the Tudeh party. He called for the shah to step down and for the establishment of an Iranian republic. The shah fled Iran. Shortly afterward, the army

Mohammed Mossadeq, first leader of Iran's National Front Party, a liberal and nonreligious group that opposed the shah in the 1950s, became Iran's prime minister and president from 1951 to 1953. This photo was taken during Mossadeq's visit to New York City in 1951.

arrested Mossadeq, who then spent three years in prison and the remainder of his life under house arrest. The shah returned and, with American help, cracked down on the opposition, destroying the power of the Majlis. Like his father before him, Muhammad Reza Shah had become an absolute ruler.

The Road to Revolution

Muhammad Reza Shah Pahlavi became one of the world's most controversial figures. Although he was determined to modernize Iran, he clung to the centuries-old traditions of absolute rule by the shahanshah—or the king of kings. He was a supporter of women's suffrage, but at the same time he rigged elections for the Majlis and made Iran's parliament almost entirely powerless. Ultimately he would cause the humiliation of the world's most powerful nation at the hands of his most bitter opponent.

The shah's first priority after the fall of the Mossadeq government was to restore stability to Iran. He did this in a very heavy-handed manner, outlawing most of Iran's political parties. In their place he established one party loyal only to him and one opposition party that was actually operated by his trusted advisers. After the lively politics of the Mossadeq era, neither of these political parties had much appeal to most Iranians. Even worse, the arrest of Mossadeq had made many Iranian people increasingly distrustful of the shah.

The Iranian economy, however, showed a marked improvement during the first years following the fall of Mossadeq. In addition to a settlement reached with the British to split the profits of the National Iranian Oil Company, Iran gained economic aid from the United States. Both the breakup of the oil profits and the injection of U.S. funds boosted the Iranian economy. The shah tried to use this to finance his modernization programs, but massive inflation caused the boom to be short-lived.

Shortly after, Iran experienced an economic downturn and increasing political repression by the shah's government. These events caused a political and fiscal crisis from 1961 to 1963. The 1960 elections for the Majlis were so obviously rigged that the shah was forced to have them canceled. Without a parliament, the government ruled by absolute decree. In 1961, the shah appointed Ali Armini, a political reformer who acted as the new prime minister. He began work on a long-overdue land reform law but was forced to resign by the shah in 1962.

The White Revolution

The following year, the shah asked the people of Iran to vote on a number of reforms, including the rethinking of land agreements and the right of women to vote. These reforms were called the Revolution of the Shah and His People, better known as the White Revolution. Discontent with the shah's rule had reached such a high level that even these essentially conservative reforms were opposed. One very dangerous source of opposition was the radical Islamic clergy of Iran. The most vocal of these clerics was the Ayatollah Khomeini. Riots occurred in all sections of Iran, especially after the arrest of Khomeini, who was later exiled from Iran.

The shah was intent on making Iran a major world power. He was a loyal ally of the United States and in return received massive military aid. By 1976, Iran had the fifth-largest army in the world, with more than 3,000 tanks. This made Iran the dominant power in the Persian Gulf region,

Ayatollah Khomeini

Trained as a member of the Islamic clergy, Ruhollah Musaui Hendi Khomeini became a religious leader who opposed Muhammad Reza Shah during the 1930s. Exiled from Iran in 1964, he fled to Iraq where he began to organize an opposition to the shah. In 1979, he led a successful overthrow and became the leader of Iran. Khomeini became Iran's *faqih*, or religious guide, and instituted strict new laws based on the religious teachings of the Koran, Islam's holy book. Despite his conservative religious views, many Iranians welcomed Khomeini's leadership, which was militantly anti-American.

This photo shows Ayatollah Khomeini after his return from exile in France, in February 1979.

causing increased tension among other Persian Gulf nations.

This concentration on military matters, however, was accompanied by political repression and economic neglect. Despite the promises of the White Revolution, the farmers of Iran continued to suffer, and many moved into the urban slums of rapidly expanding Iranian cities. Political dissent continued to be silenced, and the Iranian secret police, called the SAVAK, gained a worldwide reputation for the brutality of their methods, which included torture, drawing comparisons with the Nazi's Gestapo. Radical fundamentalist Islamic movements gained popularity in response not only to the repressive tactics of the shah's government but also to its secular nature.

In 1971, the shah led the nations of the Oil Producing and Exporting Countries (OPEC) to dramatically raise the price of oil. The money Iran made from exporting oil rapidly quadrupled. This new wealth, however, did not improve the lot of the Iranian people. Instead, it was mostly spent on increasing military arms and displaying the glory of the shah himself. Massive inflation continued to cause hardships around the country, but it only led to more repression by the shah. By 1975, he abolished all opposition parties, declaring that Iran was not a democracy. Again, Iran was ripe for revolution.

7 AN INDEPENDENT IRAN

Despite reforms, Iran's citizens continued to struggle. Many Iranians began to blame supporters of the shah, especially because he embraced Western culture and its riches while they suffered in poverty. This period in Iran was filled with civil unrest and demonstrations.

The Islamic Revolution

Ruhollah Hendi was born in 1900 in the village of Khomein in central Iran. He attended religious schools as a young man and later became an Islamic cleric, adopting the last name of Khomeini from the town of his birth.

He quickly became one of the most radical of the Islamic clerics and was among the most vocal of the shah's political critics. During the rebellions of 1963, he was arrested by the shah's government and sent into exile one year later.

This modern map shows the Islamic Republic of Iran as an independent country bordered by Armenia, Azerbaijan, and Turkmenistan to the north, to the east by Afghanistan and Pakistan, to the south by the Gulf of Oman and the Persian Gulf, and to the west by Iraq and Turkey. Though the country is often thought to be one of radical conservative thought, its people reelected Mohammad Khatami, a moderate, as Iran's president in 2001.

After Khomeini's exile, he settled in Najaf, in Iraq, just over the border from Iran. Surrounded by his followers, he formulated his own view of the most appropriate government for Iran.

In Khomeini's conservative vision, which he called an Islamic Republic, the government would operate strictly according to the most fundamental of Shiite laws. While there would be the traditional elements of a republic in his visionary government—such as an elected parliament and an elected head of state—all its decisions required approval by a council of Islamic *shiwa*, or clerics. In this way, any laws passed would be passed in accordance with Islamic law. The head of the government would be the *faqih*, or religious guide, who would be the guardian of the Islamic Republic, with the power to overrule any law.

Khomeini maintained ties with the opposition groups in Iran, and the rising dissent of Iranian citizens was encouraged and supported by him and his followers. In 1978, faced with an economic crisis and angered at Khomeini's role in organizing protests, the shah managed to have Iraq expel Khomeini. This decision proved disastrous. Relocated in Paris, France, Khomeini had even more access than before to his followers in Iran and received increased media attention.

A series of strikes in 1978, especially in the oil fields, crippled the Iranian government. The harsh response rapidly cost the shah any support he had in Iran. Most infamous was Black Friday, September 8, 1978, when the Iranian army opened fire on demonstrators. Without clear backing from the United States, the army finally announced that it would no longer protect the shah. He left Iran on January 16, 1979. On February 1, Khomeini returned to Iran. A new era was dawning.

The Aftermath of Revolution

After a brief period of putting down the remaining forces loyal to the shah, Khomeini and his followers settled down to the process of remaking Iran in their own conservative image. Though led by fundamentalists, the revolution was also influenced by the Western liberal ideology of a democratic welfare state. Many Iranians considered this influence insulting to Islam. In light of this, Khomeini's first task was to draft a new constitution.

The first draft of the constitution greatly resembled the original constitution of 1906; however, it soon included provisions for making Iran's religious leaders more powerful. Opposition to this by liberal and moderate groups in Iran was fierce, but the rise of the Iranian Revolutionary Party, the official party of Khomeini's followers, crushed much of that resistance. Then an event occurred that unified the country and swept away most of the opposition to Khomeini: the American hostage crisis.

On October 22, 1979, the United States had decided to let the former shah, who was dying of cancer, enter the country to receive

President Jimmy Carter announces the settlement of the hostage crisis on January 19, 1981. The crisis occurred during his presidential term (1977–1981) after he decided to offer sanctuary to Iran's shah after Iran was seized by Ayatollah Khomeini.

medical treatment. Angered by this, a group of Iranian students seized the U.S. Embassy in Tehran, taking sixty-six American employees hostage. The students were most likely acting with Khomeini's knowledge and the support of Iran's Revolutionary Guards, a militia force loyal only to Khomeini. Ten days later, President Jimmy Carter froze all Iranian assets in the United States.

Although the crisis helped pass the constitution Khomeini wanted and paved the way for his appointment as faqih for life, the hostage crisis became a distraction for the Islamic leader. Unfortunately, neither side could break the deadlock, especially after a disastrous attempt by the United States to rescue the hostages in April 1980, a decision that cost the lives of eight American soldiers. Even after the death of the shah that July, the hostage crisis continued. An agreement was finally reached the following year in January 1981, after Ronald Reagan had defeated Carter in the U.S. presidential election.

By then, however, Iran had greater problems than its U.S. hostages; in September of 1980, Iraq had invaded the troubled nation.

The Iran-Iraq War

Saddam Hussein, the president of Iraq, feared that the Islamic revolution of Shiite Iran would spread into his own country's Shiite population. As the leader of a secular state with

This photograph, taken in January 1981, shows just a few of the sixty-six American hostages who had been held in Tehran, Iran, as they stand during the playing of the national anthem at a welcome home ceremony on the South Lawn of the White House.

ties to the Soviet Union and Western Europe, he opposed religious revolutions of any kind. On September 22, 1980, he ordered an attack on Iran, hoping that he could exploit the chaos that its revolution had produced. He could also count on support from other Arab nations and the United States, who both wished to see the Iranian revolution contained.

Initially, the Iraqis had great success, capturing many cities along Iran's border. But the Iranian air force and navy soon responded by attacking targets in Iraq, stalling the Iraqi offensive. By 1981, the Iranians were retaking their territory, and the following year saw Iranian forces inside Iraq. Iran had seemingly won the war.

War of the Cities

But unrest among Iraq's Shiites and Khomeini's hatred of Hussein caused the Iranians to continue fighting. Iranian soldiers used the human wave attack, in which huge amounts of men attacked Iraqi positions, taking great human losses. When they ran into stiff Iraqi resistance, the war reached a stalemate.

Iraq responded by attacking Iranian ships in the Persian Gulf. In 1985, the Iraqi air force began the bombing of Iranian cities, specifically Tehran. The Iranians responded by bombing Iraqi cities in this phase of the war that was later called the "War of the Cities."

The Iran-Contra Affair

Although the Iran-Iraq War had the potential danger of drawing the world's two superpowers, the United States and the Soviet Union, into conflict, both sides maintained the stalemate. Neither superpower wanted the conflict to spill over into a larger, global war. The Soviets helped supply Iraq throughout the conflict while the United States gave Iraq valuable satellite pictures of Iranian troop

This photograph, taken in May 1991, shows the defiance of Iranian women in opposition to fundamentalist Islamic forces. Iranian women fight alongside men in the National Liberation Army of Iran, which as of 1997 was 30,000 strong. Seventy percent of the army's soldiers are female. Many are followers of Maryam Rajavi, a woman dubbed the Joan of Arc of the Muslim world because of her outspoken position against Iran's fundamentalist movement.

movements. The United States also secretly supplied Iran with anti-tank missiles on at least two occasions. Discovery of these arms shipments so soon after the hostage crisis, and despite President Reagan's vow not to negotiate with terrorists, erupted into the scandal known later as Iran-Contra. The arms sale later became a major embarrassment for the Reagan administration.

By 1987, a new phase began. Iran's acquisition of Chinese missiles that could attack ships in the Persian Gulf led to greater U.S. involvement in the region. The U.S. Navy began to escort Kuwait's oil tankers through the Persian Gulf and, on several occasions, clashed with Iranian forces. Finally, a renewed Iraqi offensive convinced the Iranians to accept a cease-fire agreement on August 20, 1988.

The Iran-Iraq War ultimately resulted in little gain for either side. At least a million people were killed, with many more wounded; millions of others were dislocated from their homes. Saddam Hussein utilized some of the worst weapons available, including poison gas and/or strategic missiles, the disastrous effects of which are still felt.

Modern Iran

By the end of the Iran-Iraq War, it was clear that Khomeini did not have much longer to live. Plans were made for finding his successor. At the same time, Khomeini ordered a revision of the constitution to remove some of the conflicts its more freehanded structure had caused.

On June 3, 1989, Ayatollah Khomeini died. He was succeeded as faqih by Ayatollah Ali Khamenei. The speaker of the Majlis, Hashemi Rafsanjani, was also elected as the new president of Iran. The revisions to the constitution gave him more power than his predecessors had, although ultimate authority still lay with the faqih.

Although Rafsanjani and Khamenei were both more moderate than Khomeini, Iran's relationship with the West, and the United States in particular, did not improve. The continued support by Khamenei and Rafsanjani of Khomeini's 1988 fatwa, or religious decree, demanding the death of the author Salman Rushdie, whose novel *The Satanic Verses* was considered blasphemous by many Muslims, did little to improve Iran's reputation with the rest of the world.

The Persian Gulf War

When the Persian Gulf War erupted in 1991 between Iraq and a coalition led by the United States, Iran remained neutral. However, Iraqi fears that Iran might take advantage of the war led them to relinquish territory gained in the Iran-Iraq conflict. It also released all prisoners of war still inside Iraq.

In the years following the Gulf War, conditions gradually improved in Iran. Although it remained an Islamic republic dominated by a radical, fundamentalist clergy, Iran never fell to the depths of other fundamentalist regimes. For example, in contrast to recent life in Afghanistan under the fundamentalist Taliban government, women in Iran still have the right to vote, may receive an education, and make up a major part of the workforce.

In 1997, in an electoral upset, a moderate candidate, Mohammad Khatami, defeated Rafsanjani in the presidential election. He urged a greater tolerance of dissent than was previously allowed and managed to improve relations with Europe. Still, it must be remembered that ultimate power does not lie with Khatami, and he has been quick to crack down on dissent whenever it seems to threaten the government.

Since the terrorist attacks on the United States of September 11, 2001, Iran has again found itself isolated. Already an opponent of the Taliban, Iran accepted many refugees from

Iranian Shiites shout anti-U.S. slogans in February 2002 at the mausoleum of the founder of the Islamic revolution, Ayatollah Ruhollah Khomeini in Tehran, Iran. The day marked the twenty-third anniversary of the Islamic revolution. United States president George W. Bush had recently reiterated his naming of "axis of evil" rogue states, calling Iran, Iraq, and North Korea the world's most dangerous enemies.

Afghanistan during the allied operations there. However, the alleged long-standing support for terrorist organizations by the Iranian government and its inclusion as a member of President George W. Bush's "axis of evil" seem to threaten the small reforms won during the last few years. Iran's course in the future will most likely remain troubled.

TIMELINE

5000 BC Mesopotamia flourishes

3300 BC Writing begins in Sumer

2500 BC Egyptians build the pyramids

2400 BC Assyrian Empire is established

2334 BC Rule of Sargon I

1750 BC Rule of Hammurabi in Babylonia

638 BC Approximate birth of Persian prophet Zoroaster (Zarathrustra)

600 BC Cyrus the Great establishes the Achaemenid Empire

563 BC Approximate birth of Buddha

331 BC Alexander the Great captures Babylon

323 BC Alexander the Great dies

AD 200 Sassanians rise to power

AD 226 Approximate date Zoroastrianism is established

AD 313 Christianity is accepted by the Romans

AD 570 Birth of Muhammad

AD 600 Roman, Parthian, and Kushan Empires flourish

AD 610 Muhammad's first revelation

AD 622 Buddhism begins its spread from India to Asia

AD 625 Muslims control Mesopotamia and Persia

AD 632 Death of Muhammad

AD 633–700 Followers of Islam start to spread their faith

AD 685 Shiite revolt in Iraq

AD 750 Abbasid caliphate, Iraq

AD 751 Arabs learn papermaking from the Chinese

AD 762 City of Baghdad is founded

AD 1215 Genghis Khan captures China and moves westward

AD 1220 Mongols sack Bukhara, Samarkand, and Tashkent

AD 1258 Mongols sack Baghdad

AD 1379 Timur invades Iraq

AD 1387 Timur conquers Persia

AD 1453 Ottoman Empire captures Constantinople and begins overtaking Asia

AD 1498 Vasco da Gama reaches India

AD 1526 Babur establishes Mughal Empire

AD 1534 Ottomans seize Iraq

AD 1554 First Russian invasion into central Asia

AD 1632 Taj Mahal is built

AD 1739 Nadir Shah invades the Mughal Empire and sacks Delhi

AD 1740 Ahmad Shah Durrani founds kingdom in Afghanistan

AD 1858 British rule is established in India

AD 1932 Saudi Arabia is founded by 'Abd al-'Aziz Al Sa'ud

AD 1947 Britain declares India's independence; succession of East and West Pakistan

AD 1979 Militant Iranian students sieze the U.S. Embassy and take American hostages

AD 1980–1988 Iran-Iraq War

AD 1997 Khatami defeats Rafsanjani in Iran's presidential election

AD 2002 Khatami recommends a settlement to the U.S. call for attacks in Iraq

GLOSSARY

abdicate To renounce a throne, high office, dignity, or function.

allied Joined together; the Allied powers was the name given to nations united against Axis powers (see below) in World War II.

Asia Minor The peninsula forming the western extremity of Asia between the Black Sea in the north, the Mediterranean Sea in the south, and the Aegean Sea in the west.

axis An alliance; name given to combined forces of Nazis, Fascists, and Japan in World War II.

ayatollah A title given to religious men with positions of leadership in the the Islamic Shiite hierarchy.

caliph A successor of Muhammad who is the secular and spiritual head of Islam.

dictatorship A form of government in which absolute power is concentrated in one person, or dictator.

exile To banish or expel a person from his or her country.

fundamentalism A movement or attitude stressing strict and literal adherence to a set of basic principles and/or religious beliefs.

Hellenism A devotion to or imitation of ancient Greek thought, customs, or styles, including classical ideas.

Islam The religious faith of Muslims, including belief in Allah as the sole deity and in Muhammad as his prophet.

khan A title denoting leadership or royalty, especially in Asia.

martial law The law administered by the military forces of an occupying power.

monotheism The belief in one god.

mosque A building used for prayer by Muslims.

Muslim A person who practices the religion of Islam.

nationalize To establish control or ownership of a company by the national government.

nomad A member of a people with no fixed residence but who roam from place to place, usually seasonally, in order to sustain themselves.

Persian One of the major language families spoken in central Asia, which includes Pashto and Tajik.

pious Reverently religious; devout.

propaganda The spread of ideas, information, or rumors for the purposes of helping or injuring an institution, a cause, or a person. Propaganda is sometimes used by governments to sway public opinion.

shah A sovereign of Iran.

Shiite Muslim sect that holds that leadership of the Islamic community should be by dynastic succession from the prophet Muhammad and his descendants.

Silk Road A series of travel routes that caravans took through central Asia linking China and India to western Europe.

suffrage The right to vote.

Sunni Muslim sect that holds that Muhammad's successor should be elected.

terrorism The use or threat of violence to create fear or alarm. The word "terrorism" first appeared during the French Revolution (1789–1799) to describe the practice of some revolutionaries.

FOR MORE INFORMATION

Asia Society and Museum
725 Park Avenue at 70th Street
New York, NY 10021
(212) 288-6400
Web site: http://www.asiasociety.org

Association for Asian Studies
1021 East Huron Street
Ann Arbor, MI 48104
(734) 665-2490
Web site: http://www.aasianst.org

Central Eurasia Project
The Open Society Institute
400 West 59th Street
New York, NY 10019
Web site: http://www.eurasianet.org

Silk Road Foundation
P.O. Box 2275
Saratoga, CA 95070
Web site: http://www.silk-road.com/
toc/index.html

Web Sites

Due to the changing nature of Internet links, the Rosen Publishing Group, Inc., has developed an online list of Web sites related to the subject of this book. This site is updated regularly. Please use this link to access the list:

http://www.rosenlinks.com/liha/iran/

FOR FURTHER READING

Cartlidge, Cherese. *Iran* (Modern Nations). Chicago, IL: Gale/Lucent Books, 2002.
Daniel, Elton L. *The History of Iran.* Westport, CT: Greenwood Press, 2001.
Fox, Mary Virginia. *Iran.* Chicago: Children's Press, 1991.

Hoge, James F., Jr. *How Did This Happen? Terrorism and the New War.* New York: Public Affairs, 2001.
Sanders, Renfield. *Iran.* Broomall, PA: Chelsea House, 1990.
Stein, R. Conrad. *The Iran Hostage Crisis.* Chicago: Children's Press, 1994.

BIBLIOGRAPHY

Daniel, Elton L. *The History of Iran.* Westport, CT: Greenwood Press, 2001.
Forbis, William H. *Fall of the Peacock Throne: The Story of Iran.* New York: Harper & Row, 1980.
Hiro, Dilip. *The Longest War: The Iran-Iraq Military Conflict.* New York: Routledge, 1991.
Mertz, Helen Chapin, ed. *Iran: A Country Study.* Washington, D.C.: Federal Research Division, 1989.

Moin, Baqer. *Khomeini: Life of the Ayatollah.* New York: St. Martin's Press, 2000.
Sciolino, Elaine. *Persian Mirrors: The Elusive Face of Iran.* New York: Touchstone Books, 2001.
Wright, Robin B. *The Last Great Revolution: Turmoil and Transformation in Iran.* New York: Vintage, 2001.

INDEX

About the Author

Fred Ramen is the author of more than twenty-five books for young adults. He lives in New York City.

Acknowledgments

Special thanks to Aisha Khan for her generous insight into Middle Eastern and Asian history and culture.

Photo Credits

Cover (map), pp. 1 (foreground), 4–5, 52–53 © 2002 Geoatlas; cover (background), pp. 1 (background), 8–9, 18–19, 38, 46, 47 courtesy of The General Libraries, The University of Texas at Austin; cover (top left), pp. 33, 49 © AKG London; cover (top right), p. 43 © Christie's Images/Corbis; cover (bottom left) © Alexander Natruskin/Reuters/Timepix; p. 4 (inset) © Dave Bartruff/Corbis; p. 6 © Farzin Malaki/Impact Photos; pp. 10–11, 20–21, 26–27, 29, 45 maps designed by Tahara Hasan; pp. 10 (inset), 22, 23 © AKG London/Erich Lessing; p. 12 © Chris Hellier/Corbis; p. 13 © Royalty-Free/Corbis; p. 14 © Dagli Orti/The Art Archive; pp. 16–17 © David Lees/Corbis; p. 24 © Christopher Bluntzer/Impact Photos; p. 26 (inset) © Robin Laurance/Impact Photos; p. 28 (top) © AKG Photos; p. 28 (bottom) © Brian A. Vikander/Corbis; p. 30 © The Art Archive; pp. 32–33, 42 © Mary Evans Picture Library; p. 34 © AKG London/British Library; p. 35 © The Art Archive/Bodleian Library Oxford/The Bodleian Library; pp. 36–37 © Historical Picture Archive/Corbis; p. 39 © The Art Archive/Palace of Chihil Soutouri Isfahan/Dagli Orti; p. 40 © Roger Wood/Corbis; pp. 44, 51, 55 © Bettmann/Corbis; p. 56 © Wally McNamee/Corbis; p. 57 © Francoise de Mulder/Corbis; p. 59 © AFP/Corbis.

Editor

Joann Jovinelly

Series Design and Layout

Tahara Hasan

Photo Research

Elizabeth Loving